I0144140

WHIMSICAL
CATS &
KITTENS

BY

ART LOVE PASSION

This book may not be reproduced in whole or in part, in any form or by any means, electronic or mechanical, including photocopying , without written permission from the publisher.

©2016 by Angelika Parker

Hello,

I'm so happy you decided to get my
Cats & Kittens coloring book.

My name is Angelika Parker and I'm the Illustrator
and Artist at Art Love Passion. Well, I basically
run this whole "operation"...lol.

I hope you will enjoy coloring these cute cats,
as much as I enjoyed doodling them.

You can use the bonus pages as backgrounds
for your own cat pictures.

Please feel free to share some of your colored pictures
with me. I'm alwas happy to see how you decided
to color these cute **Cats & Kittens**.

You can find more of my art and contact information here:

www.artlovepassion.com

Here are a few suggestions, before you begin coloring:

I would recommend using colored pencils or gel pens.

If you want to use markers, make sure to place
a blank sheet of paper between the pages.
Just in case the markers bleed through the page.

©2016 by Angelika Parker

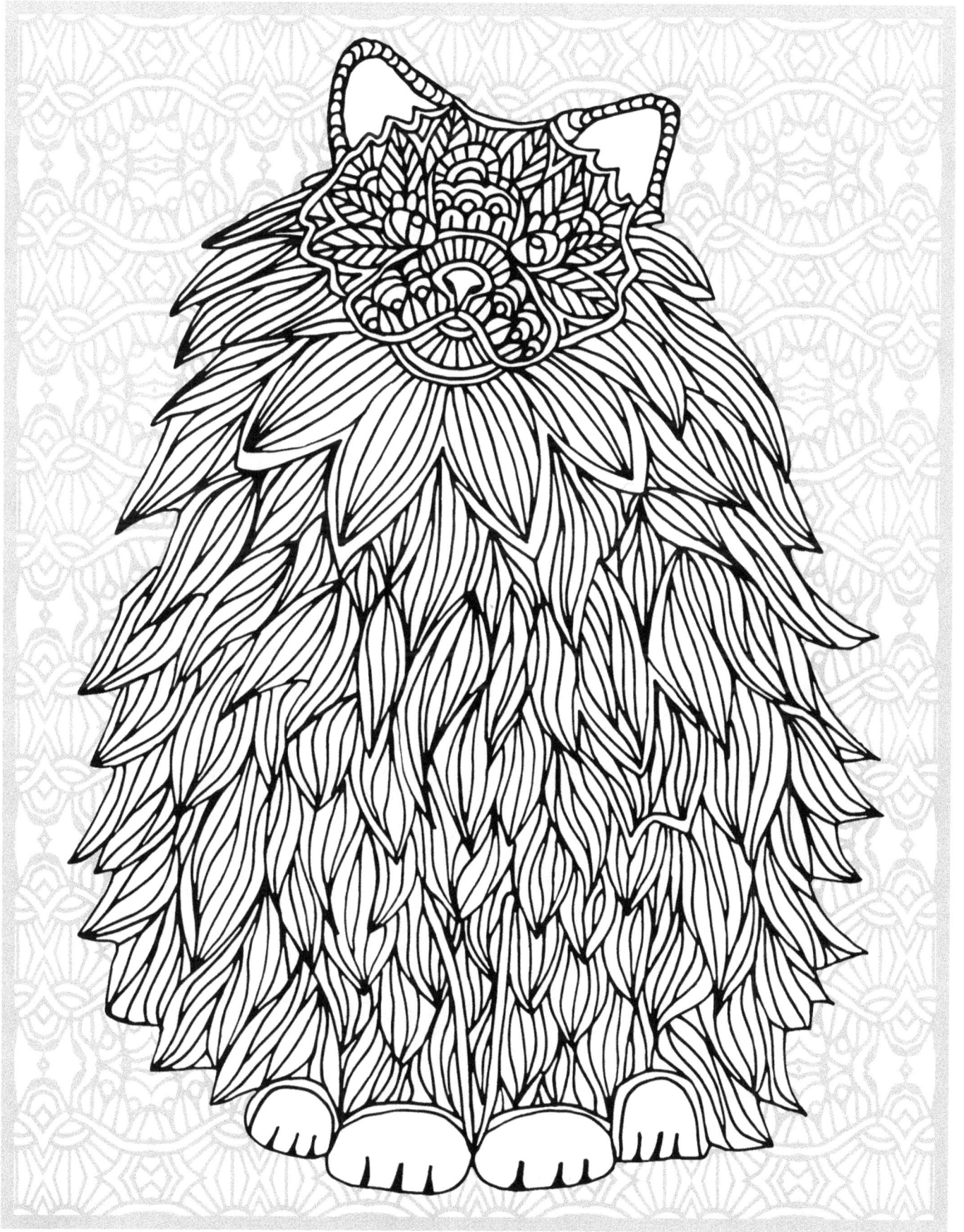

©2016 by Angelika Parker

©2016 by Angelika Parker

©2016 by Angelika Parker

©2016 by Angelika Parker

©2016 by Angelika Parker

©2016 by Angelika Parker

©2016 by Angelika Parker

©2016 by Angelika Parker

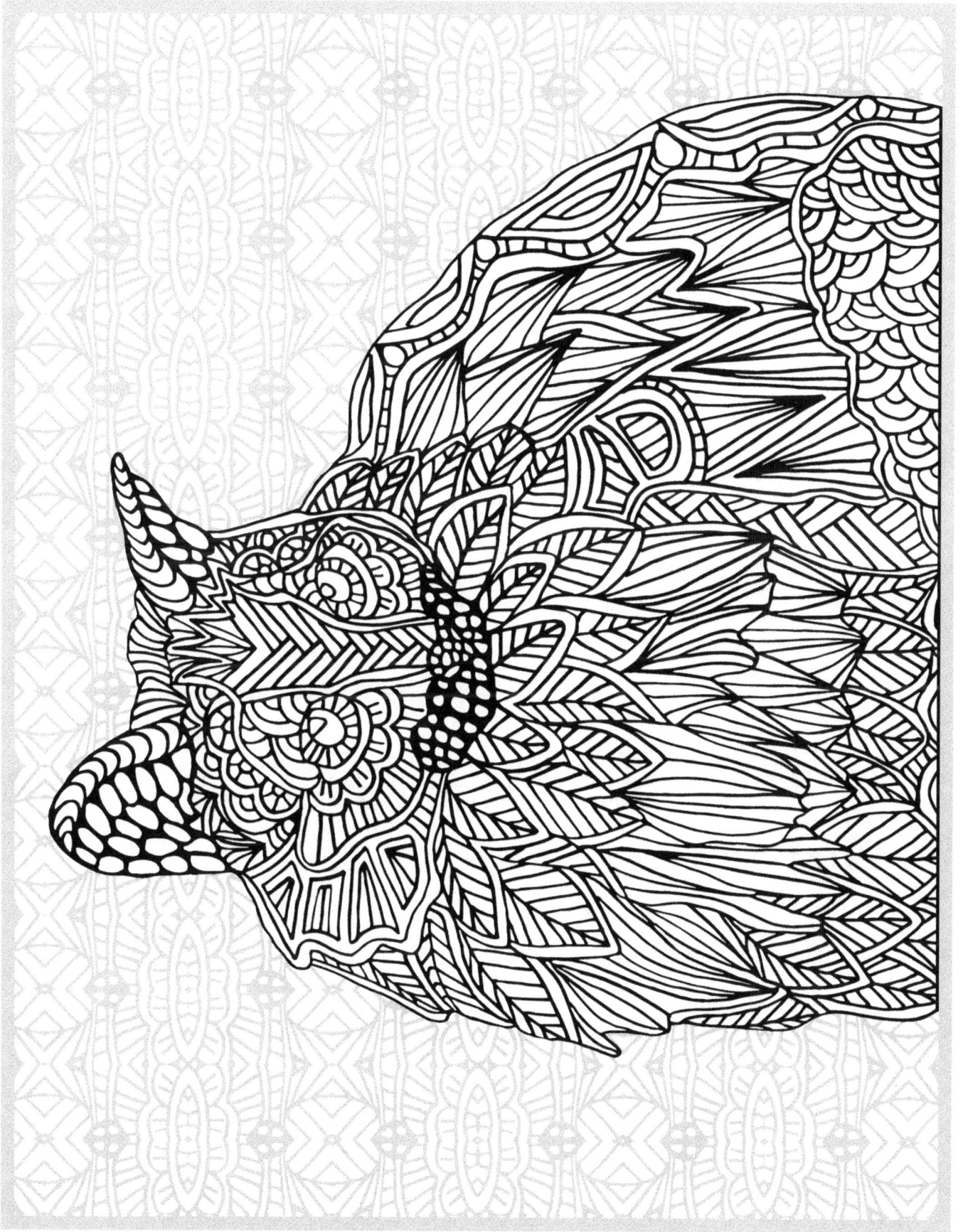

©2016 by Angelika Parker

©2016 by Angelika Parker

©2016 by Angelika Parker

©2016 by Angelika Parker

©2016 by Angelika Parker

©2016 by Angelika Parker

©2016 by Angelika Parker

©2016 by Angelika Parker

©2016 by Angelika Parker

©2016 by Angelika Parker

©2016 by Angelika Parker

©2016 by Angelika Parker

©2016 by Angelika Parker

©2016 by Angelika Parker

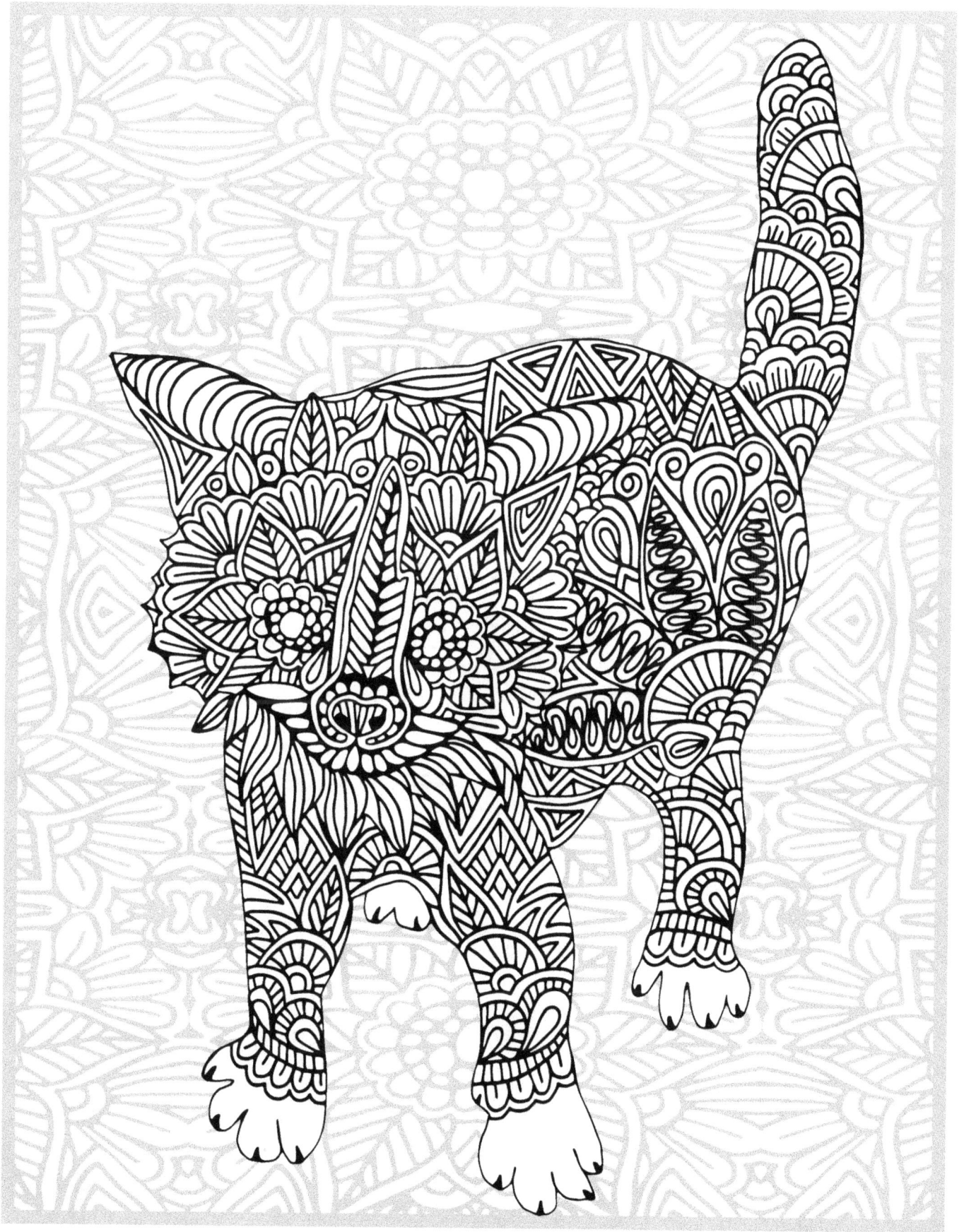

©2016 by Angelika Parker

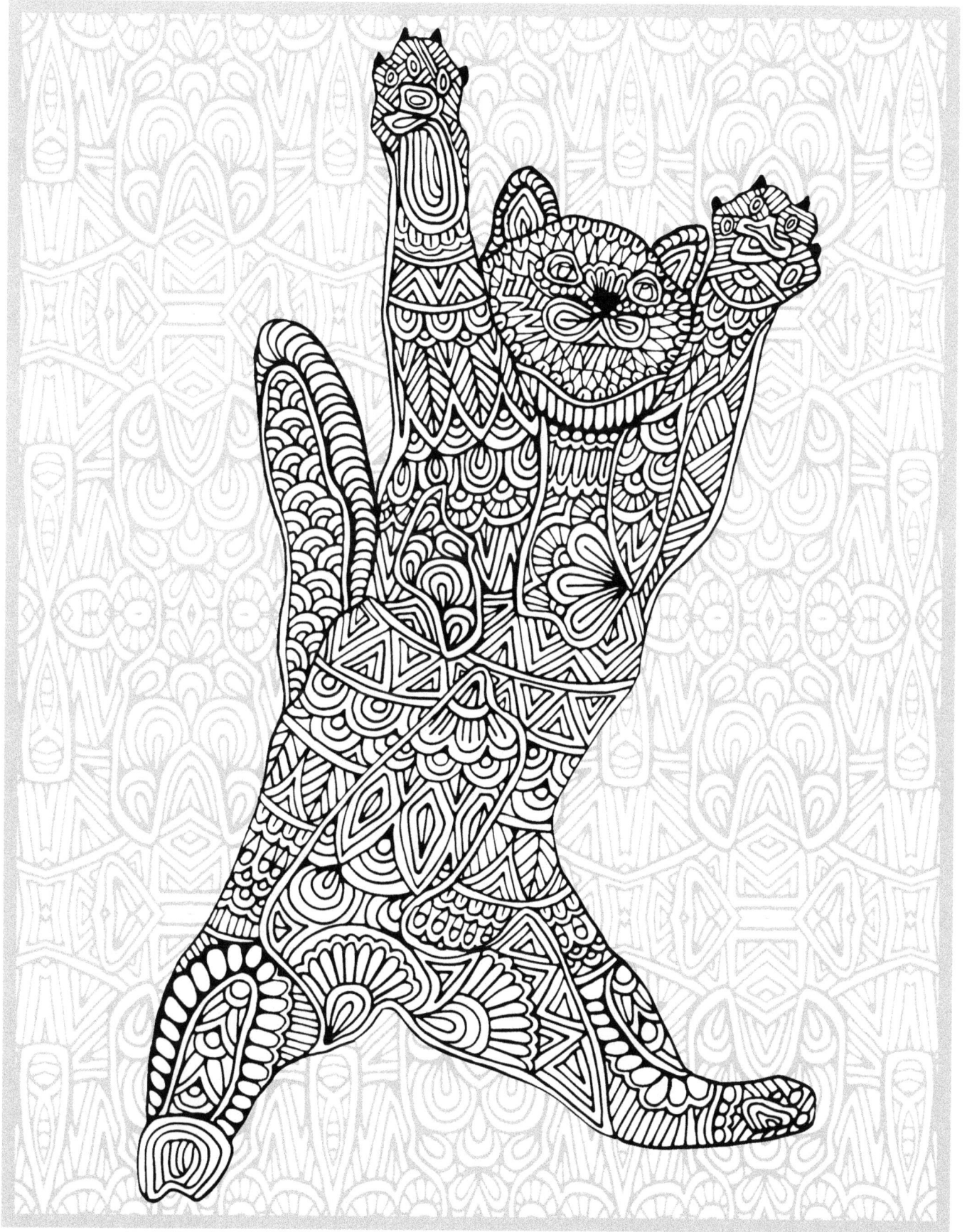

©2016 by Angelika Parker

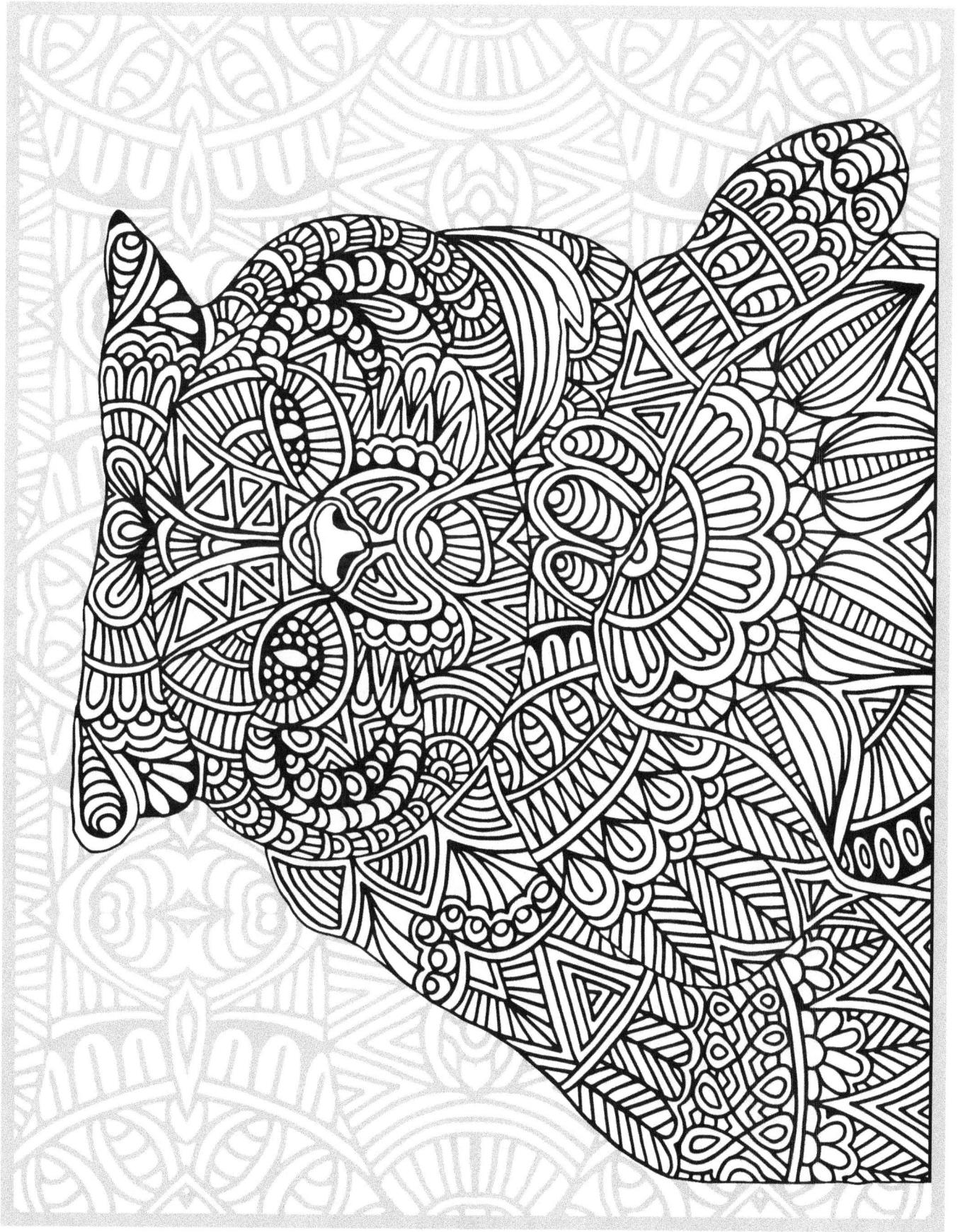

©2016 by Angelika Parker

©2016 by Angelika Parker

©2016 by Angelika Parker

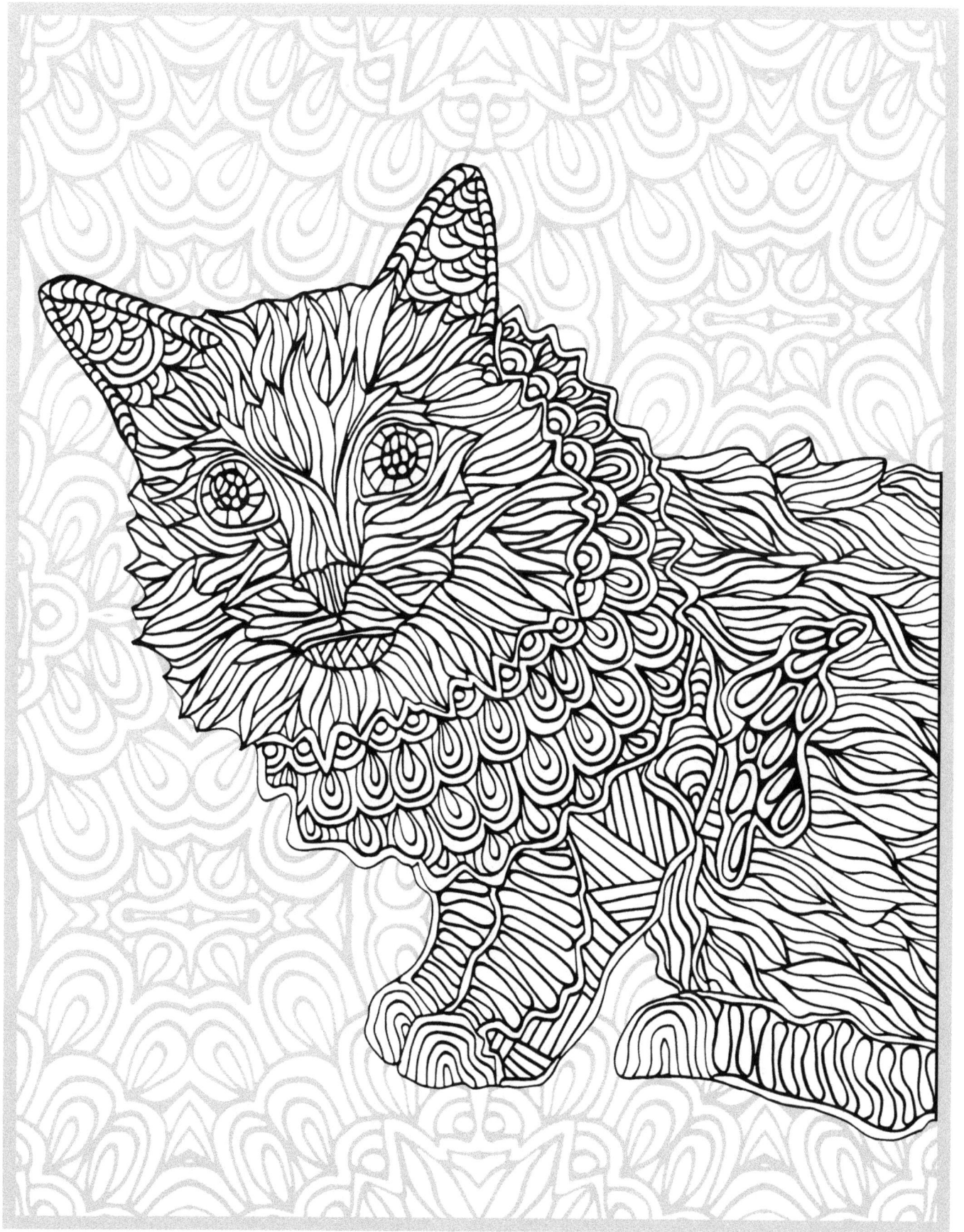

©2016 by Angelika Parker

©2016 by Angelika Parker

©2016 by Angelika Parker

©2016 by Angelika Parker

©2016 by Angelika Parker

©2016 by Angelika Parker

Looks like this is the end...
but only for this coloring book.

Follow me on social media and see what
projects I'm currently working on.

www.facebook.com/SparkysArt/
www.instagram.com/myartlovepassion
www.twitter.com/parkerangelika
www.pinterest.com/artlovepassion

If you would like to purchase more of my art, check out
my website, which has many links to my shops.

www.artlovepassion.com

You can also contact me here:

myartlovepassion@gmail.com

www.ingramcontent.com/pod-product-compliance
Lightning Source LLC
Chambersburg PA
CBHW080937040426
42443CB00015B/3443